C0-ATV-754

International Cooking Collection

High Fiber Cooking

*International
Cooking Collection*

High Fiber
Cooking

Carole Handslip

CONTENTS

Cooking Rice & Pulses   6

Breakfast Dishes   8

Soups & Appetizers   16

Light Lunches & Suppers   24

Main Course Dishes   32

Accompaniments & Salads   44

Desserts   56

Baking   66

Basic Recipes   74

High Fiber Sources   78

Index   80

Published exclusively for Cupress (Canada) Ltd
20 Torbay Road, Markham, Ontario L3R 1G6 Canada
by Woodhead-Faulkner (Publishers) Ltd, Simon & Schuster International Group

This edition first published 1988
© Woodhead-Faulkner (Publishers) Ltd 1988
All rights reserved
ISBN 0-920691-48-X
Printed and bound in Italy

INTRODUCTION

For centuries people have gone to excessive lengths to remove the fiber—or roughage, as it is also known—from the food we eat. Since Roman times millers have refined away the fiber from most of our flour to make bread as 'pure and white' as possible. So why the sudden change of heart? What is it that has transformed our thinking about fiber? What is this fiber anyway?

Fiber is an indigestible fibrous material which occurs naturally in plant foods. It is not found in animal foods. Fiber has no apparent nutritional value, for it passes through our systems virtually unchanged, yet it is an extremely valuable material, for it greatly assists the movement of foods through our digestive systems.

A simple study of the African villager's state of health shows just how valuable fiber is. Diseases such as constipation, cancer of the bowel, diverticulitis and many other 'Western ailments' that plague us in later life are relatively unknown among African village dwellers. The staple food in Africa is corn, supplemented by root crops, fruits, nuts and grains—all rich in dietary fiber. But submit the African villager to our Western diet and he finds himself prone to those 'Western diseases'.

Most experts now agree that the typical Western diet is deficient in fiber, a factor which can be detrimental to health. High fiber foods benefit us in many ways. First, fiber adds bulk to our food, giving us a sense of fullness, without having consumed a large amount of calories. So foods rich in fiber can play an important role in a calorie-controlled diet.

Fiber makes food travel faster through the intestines, exercising the lower digestive tract, reducing pressure, preventing constipation and diluting potentially harmful toxic waste substances. Another bonus is that foods rich in dietary fiber tend to be low in saturated fat, which is associated at high levels with heart disease and related disorders.

All of us eat some fiber; most of us simply don't eat nearly enough. It's not a question of rushing out to stock up with a range of new, way out foods; it's more a need to alter the balance of our eating habits.

Start by introducing wholegrain cereals at breakfast time, or make your own granola or muesli. Bake your own bread from whole wheat flour if you possibly can. Once a week I make a batch of loaves and freeze them for use during the week. If you haven't time to do this, make sure you buy whole wheat bread. Introduce a wide variety of beans, pulses and grains, vegetables and fruits, and you will certainly be increasing your fiber intake. If you also cut down on refined foods, especially sugar, add less salt to food and eat less fat, particularly animal fat, you will undoubtedly enjoy a healthier diet.

COOKING RICE & PULSES

BROWN RICE

Brown rice has an interesting nutty flavor and a chewier texture than white rice. The reason for this is that unlike white rice, brown rice has not been stripped of its fiber, the rich outer coat which also supplies us with valuable vitamins, particularly Thiamin B_1. You can buy brown long-grain, short-grain, Basmati and Italian rice. I think Basmati is the most delicious.

Brown rice is straightforward to cook; it is far less likely to go mushy than white rice, though it does entail a longer cooking time. There are two main methods of cooking brown rice; the first minimizes the loss of vitamins.

Allow ¼ cup rice per person.

Cooking Method 1

1. Wash the rice well and drain.
2. Place in a saucepan and add approximately 1 cup boiling water and a pinch of salt for each ¼ cup rice. Bring back to the boil, cover and simmer for 35–40 minutes.
3. Check after 30 minutes to make sure it is not too dry; add a little more water if necessary.
4. By the end of the cooking time, the water should have been completely absorbed and the rice should be dry and fluffy. If not, uncover and cook for 1 minute to drive off the excess moisture.

Cooking Method 2

1. Cook the rice in plenty of boiling salted water for 35–40 minutes.
2. Drain, rinse well, drain again and turn into a warmed shallow dish. Leave in a warm place for a few minutes to steam dry.

PULSES

This is the collective name for beans, peas and lentils. They are cheap to buy, keep well and are the basis of many interesting dishes, often originating from the Middle East and South America. It can be difficult to get your family to start eating beans and lentils. My advice is to introduce them gradually, first in the familiar dishes such as chili con carne, lentil soup and minestrone. After a while, the family will accept them in their more adventurous guises.

Beans are one of the richest sources of fiber; they have a high protein content and are also rich in iron, potassium and the B vitamins. When sprouted, they have the added bonus of vitamin C. One common objection to pulses is that they cause flatulence. To counter this problem, introduce them in your diet gradually and take care with their cooking. Drain off the water in which they are soaked, as this contains the substances which cause flatulence.

All dried beans and peas need to be soaked for about 8 hours, or overnight, before cooking. Alternatively, cook them in boiling water for 2 minutes, then remove from the heat and leave to soak for 2 hours. Lentils and split peas do not need to be pre-soaked before cooking, though it will shorten the cooking time if they are.

For convenience and to save energy, I tend to cook large quantities of beans when I have the time, put them in bags and freeze for future use; you can also store them in the refrigerator for 2–3 days.

Cooking Method

1. Drain the beans, place in a pan and add about 4 times their volume of fresh water; bring to the boil. Boil rapidly for 10 minutes to destroy any harmful toxins that may be present, skimming off any scum.
2. Reduce the heat, cover and simmer for the required cooking time (see page 79). Add salt, if desired, toward the end of cooking as it toughens the skin and lengthens the cooking time if added sooner.

NUTS AND SEEDS

One of the easiest and most delicious ways of increasing the fiber content of both sweet and savory dishes is to add seeds or nuts to them. The flavor of the nuts and seeds is even richer (and I find more delicious) when you roast them. Cool and add to salads, fruit dishes, muesli and savory dishes.

To brown sunflower seeds, sesame seeds and pumpkin seeds

Place the seeds in a dry heavy-based pan with a tight-fitting lid. Shake the pan over a moderate heat for about 1 minute or until the seeds begin to pop and turn golden brown.

To brown nuts

Chop the nuts if you prefer, then sprinkle them in a single layer on a baking sheet. Place in a 375°F oven for about 10 minutes or until golden brown. If you are in a hurry, broil the nuts for 4–5 minutes and turn frequently.

NOTES

All spoon measurements are level.

Ovens should be preheated to the temperature specified.

Fresh herbs are used unless otherwise stated. If unobtainable, dried herbs can be substituted in cooked dishes but halve the quantities.

If fresh yeast is unobtainable, substitute dried yeast but halve the quantity and use according to the manufacturer's directions.

Use U.S. grade large eggs unless otherwise stated.

Basic recipes are marked with an asterisk and given in the reference section (pages 74–7). Increase or decrease the basic quantities in proportion to obtain the amount required.

Freshly ground black pepper is intended where pepper is listed.

BREAKFAST DISHES

KEDGEREE

A traditional Anglo-Indian breakfast dish. Cook the rice the night before then it will only take you a few minutes to assemble and heat through. I prefer to use Finnan haddie as it is free from artificial coloring and has an excellent flavor.

Serves 4
Preparation time:
15 minutes, plus cooking rice
Cooking time:
5 minutes
Freezing:
Not recommended

1/2 cup brown rice, cooked
2 hard-boiled eggs, chopped
1 tablespoon chopped parsley

1/2 lb Finnan haddie (smoked haddock), poached and flaked
2 tablespoons sour cream
salt and pepper to taste

1. Place the rice, eggs, parsley, fish, and salt and pepper in a pan. Mix together, then heat through gently, stirring.
2. Stir in the sour cream and serve immediately.

SUNRISE SUNDAE

A fresh start to the day, but a little more filling than the citrus fruits usually served at breakfast.

1/2 cup dried apricots
1/4 lb pitted prunes
2 cups water

2 oranges
1/4 cup sour cream
1/4 cup Granola (page 10)

Serves 4
Preparation time:
10 minutes
Cooking time:
15 minutes
Freezing:
Not recommended

1. Place the apricots, prunes and water in a saucepan and bring to the boil. Cover and simmer for 15 minutes, then leave to cool, with the lid on the pan.
2. Peel the oranges and divide into segments, discarding all the pith and pits. Mix with the other fruit, then turn into 4 individual shallow dishes.
3. Top each with a spoonful of sour cream, then sprinkle with a spoonful of granola.

RASPBERRY YOGURT DRINK

Refreshing and filling—ideal when you're in a hurry. Substitute blackberries, when in season, as they are very high in fiber. Experiment with other fruits of your choice —for sweeter fruits you will probably need less honey.

¼ cup raspberries   *½ cup milk*
⅔ cup plain yogurt   *2 teaspoons honey*

Makes 2 cups
Preparation time:
5 minutes
Freezing:
Not recommended

1. Place all the ingredients in a blender or food processor, and work until smooth.
2. Pour into glasses to serve.

GRANOLA

A scrumptious cereal to serve at breakfast time with milk or plain yogurt and fruit. Alter the cereals, nuts and seeds according to what you have available. Coconut gives it an interesting flavor for a change.
I particularly like to serve granola with apricot puree —made simply by cooking ⅔ cup dried apricots in 1¼ cups water for 20 minutes, then working in a blender or food processor until smooth.

3 tablespoons sunflower   *1 cup buckwheat flakes*
*   oil*   *½ cup chopped filberts*
¼ cup malt extract   *3 tablespoons sunflower*
1 tablespoon honey   *   seeds*
1 cup rolled oats   *2 tablespoons sesame*
1 cup jumbo oats   *   seeds*

Makes 4½ cups
Preparation time:
15 minutes
Cooking time:
30–35 minutes
Freezing:
Not recommended

1. Place the oil, malt extract and honey in a large saucepan and heat gently until the malt is runny.
2. Stir in the remaining ingredients and mix thoroughly.
3. Turn the mixture into a large roasting pan and bake in a 350°F oven for 30–35 minutes, stirring occasionally so that it browns evenly.
4. Leave to cool, breaking up the granola to separate the pieces as it does so. Store in an airtight container.

VARIATION
Mix together 1 cup granola, ⅔ cup plain yogurt, and 1 sliced banana or 2 sliced peaches and divide between 4 individual bowls.

CORN FRITTERS

So quick to make that you don't need to get up before anyone else in the family. Vary the fritters by adding cooked diced bacon, chopped scallions or herbs.

2 tablespoons whole wheat flour
1 egg
3 tablespoons milk
1/2 cup grated Cheddar cheese

7 oz can whole kernel corn, drained
salt and pepper to taste
salad oil for shallow-frying

Makes 6
Preparation time:
15 minutes
Cooking time:
8 minutes
Freezing:
Not recommended

1. Place the flour in a mixing bowl, make a well in the center and drop in the egg. Add the milk and mix, gradually incorporating the flour; beat until smooth.
2. Mix in the cheese, corn, and salt and pepper.
3. Heat the oil in a frying pan, add tablespoonfuls of the mixture and fry for 2 minutes on each side, until golden brown. Repeat with remaining batter.

BREAKFAST BISCUITS

Very quick to make fresh for breakfast. Serve with sweet or savory toppings: try cottage cheese with chopped dates, banana or apple if you want a sweet topping; cooked diced bacon or scallions for a savory one.

2 cups whole wheat flour
1 teaspoon cream of tartar, sifted
1/2 teaspoon baking soda, sifted
pinch of salt

1/4 cup margarine
1/2 cup milk (approximately)
1/4 teaspoon poppy seeds
milk to glaze

Makes 5
Preparation time:
15 minutes
Cooking time:
12–15 minutes
Freezing:
Recommended

1. Place all the ingredients, except the poppy seeds, in a mixing bowl and mix with a fork to form a soft dough, adding a little more milk if necessary.
2. Turn onto a lightly floured surface, knead lightly and roll out to a 3/4 inch thickness. Cut into 3 inch rounds with a plain cutter.
3. Place on a floured baking sheet, brush with milk and sprinkle with the poppy seeds.
4. Bake in a 425°F oven for 12–15 minutes.
5. Transfer to a rack to cool.

MUESLI

The base mixture can be varied daily by adding grated apple or other fresh fruits. Use apple juice instead of milk for a change, and add yogurt or sour cream.

1¾ cups rolled oats
1 cup wheat flakes
1 cup barley flakes
¾ cup chopped filberts,
browned

⅔ cup golden raisins
½ cup chopped dates
½ cup chopped dried apple
2 tablespoons dark brown
sugar

Makes 1½ lb
Preparation time:
15 minutes
Freezing: Not
recommended

1. Mix all the ingredients together in a large bowl. Store in an airtight container and use as required.

FRUIT WITH NUT SAUCE

A lovely breakfast to serve in the summer when there are so many fresh fruits available. Choose several types, thinking about their color, so they will look attractive on the plate. Serve with whole wheat bread.

¹/₃ cup filberts, browned
¹/₂ cup whole wheat
  breadcrumbs
1 tablespoon honey
1 tablespoon lemon juice

³/₄ cup sour cream
  (approximately)
selection of fresh fruits in
  season (e.g. pineapple,
  watermelon, peaches,
  apples, oranges, pears)

Serves 4
Preparation time:
20–30 minutes
Freezing:
Recommended for
sauce only

1. Grind the filberts finely in a food processor.
2. Add the remaining ingredients, except the fruit, and blend until smooth; add extra sour cream to thin if necessary.
3. Prepare the chosen fruits as necessary, slice and arrange on individual plates, then spoon a little nut sauce onto each plate.

WAFFLES

These waffles are light and airy, and delicious served with
fruit puree or strawberries and yogurt.

³⁄₄ cup whole wheat flour	*1 egg, separated*
1 teaspoon cinnamon	*1 teaspoon honey*
1¹⁄₂ teaspoons baking	*1 tablespoon salad oil*
* powder*	*1 cup milk*

1. Place the flour in a mixing bowl and sift in the cinnamon and baking powder. Make a well in the center.
2. Add the egg yolk, honey, oil and milk and beat until completely smooth.
3. Whisk the egg white until fairly stiff, then fold carefully into the batter.
4. Spoon a quarter of the mixture into a heated and oiled non-stick waffle iron and cook for 2–3 minutes, until crisp and golden. Remove and keep warm.
5. Cook the remaining batter in the same way.

Makes 4
Preparation time:
10 minutes
Cooking time:
8–12 minutes
Freezing:
Recommended

BEAN AND TOMATO SOUP

A hearty, warming soup. For a quicker soup, use two 14 oz cans of drained white kidney beans instead of the dried beans; reduce the water to 4 cups and the cooking time to 30 minutes.

2 tablespoons salad oil
1 large onion, chopped
2 celery sticks, chopped
2 cloves garlic, crushed
1¼ cups navy beans, soaked overnight
1 bouquet garni
1 tablespoon tomato paste

14 oz can chopped tomatoes
5 cups water
2 teaspoons lemon juice
2 tablespoons chopped parsley
salt and pepper to taste

Serves 6–8
Preparation time:
10 minutes
Cooking time:
2 hours
Freezing:
Recommended

1. Heat the oil in a pan, add the onion and celery and fry until softened.
2. Add the garlic, drained beans, bouquet garni, tomato paste, tomatoes and water. Bring to the boil, cover and simmer for about 2 hours, until the beans are tender, adding salt and pepper toward the end of cooking time.
3. Remove the bouquet garni. Add the lemon juice and parsley, check the seasoning and pour into a warmed soup tureen.

CURRIED LENTIL SOUP

1 onion, chopped
1 celery stick, chopped
1 carrot, chopped
1 clove garlic, crushed
¾ cup red lentils
3¾ cups water

1 teaspoon curry powder
1 teaspoon turmeric
salt and pepper to taste
1 tablespoon chopped parsley to garnish

Serves 4–6
Preparation time:
10 minutes
Cooking time:
45 minutes
Freezing:
Recommended

1. Place all the ingredients, except the salt and pepper, in a large saucepan. Bring to the boil, cover and simmer for 45 minutes, stirring occasionally.
2. Add salt and pepper, pour into a warmed soup tureen and sprinkle with the parsley to serve.

RED PEPPER SOUP

A light, refreshing soup—delicious hot or cold with crunchy curls of Whole Wheat Melba Toast (page 22) or Poppy Seed Rolls (page 72).

4 red peppers
1 tablespoon sunflower oil
1 onion, chopped
1 clove garlic, crushed
2½ cups water

2 cups tomato juice
salt and pepper to taste
¼ cup sour cream to
  garnish

Serves 4
Preparation time:
25 minutes
Freezing:
Recommended

1. Plunge the red peppers into a pan of boiling water and leave to stand for 4 minutes. Drain.
2. Halve and core the peppers, removing all the seeds. Chop the flesh roughly and place in a food processor or blender.
3. Heat the oil in a pan, add the onion and fry until softened. Add the garlic and fry for 1 minute.
4. Add to the food processor or blender with the water and work until smooth.
5. Mix with the tomato juice and season with salt and pepper. Chill until required. If serving hot, heat through gently.
6. Pour into individual soup bowls and swirl a spoonful of sour cream into each one.

ICED LETTUCE SOUP

A delicately flavored soup—an ideal way to use up tough outer leaves or lettuces that may have bolted in your garden. It can be served hot if you prefer.

1 tablespoon salad oil	*3 cups milk*
1 onion, chopped	*pinch of grated nutmeg*
2 large lettuces, shredded	*²/₃ cup whipping cream*
2 tablespoons whole wheat	*salt and pepper to taste*
flour	

1. Heat the oil in a pan, add the onion and lettuce, cover and cook gently for about 8 minutes.
2. Remove from the heat and stir in the flour. Bring the milk to the boil, then gradually add to the pan, stirring constantly. Add salt, pepper and nutmeg, cover and simmer for 20 minutes.
3. Cool the soup, then puree in a food processor or blender until smooth.
4. Reserve 4 tablespoons cream for garnish. Stir the rest of the cream into the soup, then place in the refrigerator to chill. If serving hot, heat through gently, without boiling.
5. Pour into individual soup bowls and swirl the remaining cream into each one. Serve with Whole Wheat Melba Toast (page 22) or Poppy Seed Rolls (page 72).

Serves 4
Preparation time: 10 minutes
Cooking time: 30 minutes
Freezing: Recommended

MINTED MELON SALAD

A wonderful combination of flavors that makes a light, refreshing first course and excites the appetite.

1 small honeydew melon, halved	*¼ cucumber*
1 cup sliced strawberries	*2 teaspoons lemon juice*
1 tablespoon chopped mint	*1 tablespoon olive oil*
	pepper to taste

Serves 4
Preparation time:
15 minutes, plus
marinating
Freezing:
Not recommended

1. Scoop out the seeds from the melon and discard. Cut off the skin, then cut the melon into ½ inch pieces or scoop into balls, using a melon baller.
2. Place the melon in a bowl with the strawberries and sprinkle with the mint.
3. Slice the cucumber, then cut the slices into quarters. Add to the bowl.
4. Mix the lemon juice, oil and pepper together, pour over the salad and toss until well coated.
5. Leave for 30 minutes for the flavors to combine, then serve in individual dishes.

PROVENCALE SALAD

1 small eggplant, sliced	*2 tablespoons chopped parsley*
¼ cup olive oil	*⅓ cup black olives, halved and pitted*
1¾ cups sliced zucchini	
1 red pepper, cored, seeded and sliced	*1 tablespoon lemon juice*
2 cloves garlic, crushed	*salt and pepper to taste*
4 tomatoes, sliced	

Serves 6
Preparation time:
15 minutes, plus
standing and
cooling time
Cooking time:
20 minutes
Freezing:
Recommended,
without the
tomatoes

1. Place the eggplant in a colander, sprinkle with salt and leave for 30 minutes. Rinse well and pat dry with paper towels.
2. Heat half the oil in a frying pan, add the eggplant slices and fry on both sides until pale golden. Place in a bowl.
3. Add the remaining oil to the pan and fry the zucchini and red pepper for 8–10 minutes, stirring occasionally, until softened.
4. Add the garlic, and salt and pepper; fry for 2 minutes.
5. Add to the eggplant with the tomatoes, parsley, olives and lemon juice and toss thoroughly. Leave to cool, then transfer to a shallow serving dish and serve with Poppy Seed Rolls (page 72).

CASHEW NUT PATÉ

1 tablespoon salad oil
1 cup chopped mushrooms
1 clove garlic, crushed
²⁄₃ cup cashew nuts, roasted
handful parsley

³⁄₄ cup cooked pinto beans
2 tablespoons plain yogurt
salt and pepper to taste
radish slices to garnish

Serves 4–6
Preparation time:
15 minutes, plus
cooking beans
Freezing:
Recommended

1. Heat the oil in a pan, add the mushrooms and garlic and fry for 2–3 minutes, stirring occasionally. Set aside.
2. Place the nuts and parsley in a food processor or blender and chop. Add the beans and yogurt and work until smooth.
3. Turn the mixture into a bowl, add the mushrooms, and salt and pepper and mix well.
4. Turn into a serving dish, garnish with the radish slices and serve with Whole Wheat Melba Toast (see below).

MUSHROOM PATÉ

1 tablespoon sunflower oil
1 onion, chopped
¹⁄₃ lb mushrooms, chopped
2 cloves garlic, crushed
³⁄₄ cup cooked lima beans

2 tablespoons chopped
*   parsley*
¹⁄₄ teaspoon chopped
*   thyme*
salt and pepper to taste
thyme sprigs to garnish

Serves 4
Preparation time:
15 minutes, plus
cooking beans
Cooking time:
10 minutes
Freezing:
Recommended

1. Heat the oil in a pan, add the onion and fry until softened.
2. Add the mushrooms and garlic and fry for 5 minutes, stirring occasionally.
3. Puree the beans and herbs in a food processor or blender.
4. Mix with the mushroom mixture and season with salt and pepper. Turn into a serving dish and garnish with thyme. Serve with Whole Wheat Melba Toast (see below).

WHOLE WHEAT MELBA TOAST
Simply toast a slice of whole wheat bread on both sides. Place on a flat surface, cut off the crusts and, holding your hand firmly on top, split the slice horizontally with a knife, using a sawing action. Broil, cut sides up, until the toasts curl up and turn golden.

SUNFLOWER-STUFFED POTATOES

2 large potatoes
1 cup grated Cheddar
    cheese
3 tablespoons plain yogurt

6 scallions, chopped
$^1/_2$ cup sunflower seeds,
    chopped and toasted
salt and pepper to taste

Serves 4
Preparation time:
10 minutes
Cooking time:
1½ hours
Freezing:
Recommended

1. Make a slit along one side of each potato and bake in a 400°F oven for 1¼ hours or until cooked.
2. Halve the potatoes lengthways, scoop out the flesh into a bowl and mash with half the cheese, the yogurt, scallions, sunflower seeds, and salt and pepper.
3. Spoon the mixture into the potato shells, sprinkle with the remaining cheese and return to the oven for 15 minutes or until golden.

CHEESE AND CORN TART

1 tablespoon salad oil
1 onion, chopped
1 celery stick, chopped
1 clove garlic, crushed
2 eggs
$^2/_3$ cup milk
1 cup frozen whole kernel
    corn

1 cup grated Cheddar
    cheese
2 tablespoons chopped
    parsley
6 oz Whole Wheat Pastry*
salt and pepper to taste

Serves 4–6
Preparation time:
20 minutes, plus
pastry making
Cooking time:
45 minutes
Freezing:
Recommended

1. Heat the oil in a pan, add the onion, celery and garlic and fry until softened.
2. Beat the eggs and milk together in a bowl, then stir in the corn, onion mixture, cheese, parsley, and salt and pepper.
3. Roll out the pastry thinly and use to line an 8 inch pie plate.
4. Spoon in the filling and bake in a 400°F oven for 30 minutes. Lower the heat to 375°F and cook for 15 minutes. Serve warm or cold.

CHEESE ROULADE

A very impressive dish to serve with a crisp salad for a summer lunch. It is equally good eaten cold. It also makes an attractive first course served with Tomato Sauce*.

*1 cup whole wheat
   breadcrumbs*
*3/4 cup grated Cheddar
   cheese*
*1/3 cup grated Parmesan
   cheese*
*1/2 cup cream cheese
   whipped with 2
   tablespoons lemon
   juice*
4 eggs, separated
1/2 teaspoon dry mustard
salt and pepper to taste

FOR THE FILLING:
1 tablespoon salad oil
1 onion, chopped
*1/2 lb frozen chopped
   spinach, thawed and
   drained*
*1/2 cup cream cheese
   whipped with 2
   tablespoons lemon
   juice*
*good pinch of grated
   nutmeg*

Serves 4
Preparation time:
20 minutes
Cooking time:
10–15 minutes
Freezing:
Not recommended

1. Line and grease a 12 × 8 inch jelly roll pan.
2. Place the breadcrumbs, Cheddar cheese, all but 1 tablespoon of the Parmesan cheese, the cream cheese mixture, egg yolks, mustard, and salt and pepper in a bowl and mix well.
3. Whisk the egg whites until fairly stiff, then carefully fold into the cheese mixture with a metal spoon.
4. Turn the mixture into the prepared pan and bake in a 400°F oven for 10–15 minutes, until risen and firm.
5. Meanwhile, prepare the filling. Heat the oil in a pan, add the onion and fry until softened. Add the spinach and cook, stirring, for 5 minutes.
6. Add the cream cheese mixture, nutmeg, and salt and pepper and heat through gently.
7. Sprinkle the remaining Parmesan cheese over a sheet of waxed paper. Turn the roulade out onto the paper and peel off the lining paper.
8. Spread with the filling and roll up like a jelly roll. Serve immediately in slices.

VARIATIONS

Mushroom Filling: Add 1/3 lb thinly sliced mushrooms in place of the spinach and fry for 5 minutes. Continue as above.

Corn Filling: Add 2/3 cup whole kernel corn instead of the spinach and heat through gently before adding the cream cheese mixture and seasonings.

TAGLIATELLE WITH OLIVE SAUCE

*1 lb fresh whole wheat
tagliatelle*
FOR THE SAUCE:
1 tablespoon olive oil
1 onion, sliced
*1 red pepper, cored, seeded
and sliced*
2 cloves garlic, crushed

*14 oz can chopped
tomatoes*
½ teaspoon dried oregano
⅓ cup olives, pitted
salt and pepper to taste
TO SERVE:
grated Parmesan cheese

1. First, prepare the sauce. Heat the oil in a pan, add the onion and red pepper and cook gently for 5 minutes, stirring occasionally. Add the remaining ingredients and cook for 5 minutes.
2. Cook the tagliatelle according to package directions, drain well, then turn into a warmed serving dish.
3. Pour over the sauce and sprinkle with Parmesan cheese, or hand it separately, to serve.

Serves 4
Preparation time:
10 minutes
Cooking time:
10 minutes
Freezing:
Recommended for
sauce only

TOMATO AND EGGPLANT CREPES

1 large eggplant, diced
1 tablespoon olive oil
1 clove garlic, crushed
14 oz can chopped
  tomatoes
1 tablespoon chopped
  parsley

12 Whole Wheat Crepes*
2 tablespoons grated
  Parmesan cheese
salt and pepper to taste
cilantro sprigs to garnish

Serves 4–6
Preparation time:
20 minutes, plus
standing time and
making crepes
Cooking time:
15 minutes
Freezing:
Recommended

1. Place the eggplant in a colander, sprinkle with salt and leave for 30 minutes. Rinse and dry with paper towels.
2. Heat the oil in a pan, add the eggplant and fry until golden, turning occasionally.
3. Add the garlic and fry for 1 minute, then add the tomatoes, parsley, and salt and pepper. Cover and simmer for 10 minutes, stirring occasionally.
4. Divide the filling between the crepes, roll up and place in a lightly oiled, shallow ovenproof dish.
5. Sprinkle with the Parmesan cheese and bake in a 375°F oven for 15 minutes, until heated through. Garnish with cilantro. Serve with a salad.

BEAN AND BACON FRITTATA

This recipe is Mexican in origin and is an excellent way of using left-over beans—any variety will do.

1 tablespoon salad oil
1 onion, chopped
1 celery stick, chopped
1/3 cup chopped smoked
  bacon
4 eggs

2 tablespoons water
2 tablespoons chopped
  parsley
3/4 cup cooked pinto beans
salt and pepper to taste
salad oil for shallow-frying

Serves 2
Preparation time:
10 minutes, plus
cooking beans
Cooking time:
10–15 minutes
Freezing:
Not recommended

1. Heat the oil in a pan, add the onion, celery and bacon and fry for about 5 minutes, stirring.
2. Beat the eggs and water together in a bowl, then stir in the parsley, beans, onion mixture, and salt and pepper.
3. Heat the oil in a 9 inch frying pan, pour in the egg mixture and cook slowly for 4 minutes, until the frittata is beginning to set.
4. Remove from the heat and broil for about 2 minutes, to finish cooking.
5. Slide onto a warmed serving dish and cut into wedges.

ZUCCHINI CRUMBLE

A good way to use up large zucchini.

2 tablespoons salad oil
2 onions, sliced
5 cups sliced zucchini
2 cloves garlic, crushed
14 oz can chopped
*   tomatoes*
1 teaspoon dried oregano
1 tablespoon tomato paste
salt and pepper to taste

FOR THE CRUMBLE:
1¼ cups whole wheat
*   flour*
2 tablespoons margarine
½ cup finely grated
*   Cheddar cheese*
⅓ cup grated Parmesan
*   cheese*

Serves 4
Preparation time:
35 minutes
Cooking time:
30 minutes
Freezing:
Not recommended

1. Heat the oil in a pan, add the onions and zucchini and fry for 10 minutes, stirring occasionally.
2. Add the garlic, tomatoes, oregano, tomato paste, and salt and pepper. Cover and simmer for 10 minutes, then turn into a 1½ quart ovenproof dish.
3. To make the crumble, put the flour into a mixing bowl and rub in the margarine until the mixture resembles breadcrumbs. Stir in the cheeses.
4. Sprinkle over the zucchini mixture and bake in a 400°F oven for 30 minutes, until golden brown.

SPINACH TARTS

10 oz Whole Wheat Pastry*
1 tablespoon salad oil
1 onion, chopped
2 cloves garlic, crushed
1 lb frozen chopped
    spinach, thawed
¼ cup milk
2 eggs

½ teaspoon grated
    nutmeg
¾ cup Ricotta cheese
2 tablespoons grated
    Parmesan cheese
1 tablespoon sesame seeds
salt and pepper to taste

1. Divide the pastry into 6 pieces. Roll out one piece on a floured surface and use to line a 4 inch fluted pie plate. Repeat with the remaining pastry. Chill in the refrigerator while making the filling.
2. Heat the oil in a pan, add the onion and fry until softened. Add the garlic and spinach and cook gently for 10 minutes, stirring occasionally.
3. Cool slightly, then beat in the milk, eggs, nutmeg, cheeses, and salt and pepper.
4. Divide the filling between the tart cases and sprinkle with the sesame seeds. Place on a baking sheet and bake in a 400°F oven for 35–40 minutes, until firm. Serve warm or cold.

Serves 6
Preparation time:
20 minutes, plus
pastry making
Cooking time:
35–40 minutes
Freezing:
Recommended

MAIN COURSE DISHES

MINT FRICADELLES

Bulgur wheat is used as the base for these minty meatballs.
Serve with Tomato Sauce* and whole wheat pasta.

1/3 cup bulgur wheat
1/2 lb ground lamb
1 onion, chopped finely
1 clove garlic, crushed
*2 tablespoons chopped
    mint*

1 egg
2 teaspoons soy sauce
*3 tablespoons whole wheat
    flour*
salt and pepper to taste
salad oil for shallow-frying

Serves 4
Preparation time:
15 minutes, plus
soaking time
Cooking time:
8 minutes
Freezing:
Recommended

1. Soak the bulgur wheat for 30 minutes; drain well. Wrap
in a clean cloth and squeeze out all the moisture.
2. Place in a bowl with the remaining ingredients, except
the flour, and mix together thoroughly.
3. Using dampened hands, shape the mixture into balls
the size of a golf ball and roll in the flour.
4. Fry for about 8 minutes, turning occasionally. Drain on
paper towels and serve immediately.

SHRIMP WITH ALMONDS

An attractive stir-fry dish that only takes minutes to cook.
Serve with brown rice or Japanese egg noodles.

1 tablespoon sesame oil
1 onion, sliced
3/4 cup slivered almonds
*1 teaspoon chopped fresh
    root ginger*
1 clove garlic, crushed
*1/2 lb fresh or frozen
    snow peas*

*3/4 lb medium-size
    shelled shrimp*
2 tablespoons dry sherry
1 tablespoon soy sauce
2 tablespoons water
salt and pepper to taste

Serves 4
Preparation time:
8 minutes
Cooking time:
7 minutes
Freezing:
Not recommended

1. Heat the oil in a wok, add the onion and almonds and
stir-fry over a high heat for 1 minute.
2. Add the ginger, garlic and snow peas and stir-fry for
2 minutes.
3. Add the remaining ingredients and stir-fry for 3
minutes, then serve immediately.

KEBABS WITH BULGUR PILAFF

Bulgur wheat takes far less time to cook than other grains because it is cracked and partly cooked already, so it is very useful when you are in a rush.

KEBABS:
1 tablespoon olive oil
2 tablespoons lemon juice
1 tablespoon soy sauce
1 clove garlic, crushed
1 teaspoon chopped rosemary
1 lb lean lamb, boned and cut into 1 inch cubes
1 large red pepper, cored, seeded and cut into 1 inch squares

3 small onions, each cut into 8 pieces
BULGUR PILAFF:
1 cup bulgur wheat
1 tablespoon salad oil
1 onion, chopped
1 red pepper, cored, seeded and diced
1/4 lb mushrooms, sliced
1 tablespoon chopped parsley
1 tablespoon soy sauce

Serves 4
Preparation time:
15 minutes, plus marinating
Cooking time:
20 minutes
Freezing:
Not recommended

1. For the kebabs, mix together the oil, lemon juice, soy sauce, garlic and rosemary, pour over the meat and leave to marinate for 2 hours, turning occasionally.
2. Thread alternate pieces of lamb, red pepper and onion onto 8 skewers, then baste with the marinade.
3. Broil for 8 minutes, turning and basting frequently.
4. For the pilaff, cook the bulgur wheat in boiling salted water for 10 minutes, or until tender; drain well.
5. Heat the oil in a pan, add the onion and red pepper and fry for 5 minutes. Add the mushrooms and cook for 2 minutes, stirring.
6. Stir in the bulgur wheat, parsley and soy sauce. Turn into a serving dish and arrange the kebabs on top.

RUSSIAN FISH PIE

1 tablespoon salad oil
1 onion, chopped
1/4 lb mushrooms, sliced
1/4 cup brown rice, cooked
2 tablespoons chopped parsley

3/4 lb Finnan haddie (smoked haddock), cooked and flaked
12 oz Whole Wheat Pastry*
salt and pepper to taste
beaten egg to glaze

1. Heat the oil in a pan, add the onion and fry until softened. Add the mushrooms and fry, stirring, for 3–4 minutes.

2. Add to the rice with the parsley, haddock, and salt and pepper.

3. Divide the pastry in half and roll out one piece to form a rectangle 12 × 7 inches.

4. Place on a baking sheet and cover with the filling, leaving a 1 inch border all the way round; dampen these edges.

5. Roll out the remaining pastry slightly larger than the first piece. Cover the filling and trim the edges to fit. Press together, pinch the edges to seal and make 2 holes in the top. Decorate with leaves cut from the trimmings.

6. Brush with beaten egg and bake in a 400°F oven for 30 minutes, until golden. Serve with Watercress Sauce*.

Serves 4–6
Preparation time: 30 minutes, plus pastry making, and cooking rice and fish
Cooking time: 30 minutes
Freezing: Recommended

TOMATO AND NUT CANNELLONI

This cannelloni has a rich nutty filling which blends well with the creamy sauce. The filling also makes a good sauce to go with whole wheat tagliatelle if you add a little stock or tomato juice to thin it down.

8 whole wheat cannelloni shells
FOR THE FILLING:
1 tablespoon sunflower oil
1 onion, chopped
1 celery stick, chopped
1 tablespoon whole wheat flour
1 clove garlic, crushed
14 oz can chopped tomatoes
1/4 lb mushrooms, sliced
1 tablespoon tomato paste
1 teaspoon soy sauce
1/2 teaspoon dried oregano

3/4 cup finely chopped filberts
2 tablespoons chopped parsley
salt and pepper to taste
FOR THE SAUCE:
2 tablespoons sunflower oil
2 tablespoons whole wheat flour
1 1/4 cups milk
pinch of grated nutmeg
2 tablespoons grated Parmesan cheese
TO GARNISH:
sage or parsley sprigs

Serves 4
Preparation time:
35 minutes
Cooking time:
15–20 minutes
Freezing:
Recommended, at end of stage 6

1. Cook the pasta according to package instructions. Drain, spread on paper towels and pat dry.
2. For the filling, heat the oil in a pan, add the onion and celery and fry gently until softened.
3. Stir in the flour, then add the garlic, tomatoes, mushrooms, tomato paste, soy sauce, oregano, and salt and pepper.
4. Bring to the boil, lower the heat and simmer for 8–10 minutes. Stir in the filberts and parsley.
5. Spoon a tablespoon of filling into each cannelloni shell.
6. For the sauce, heat the oil in a pan, then stir in the flour. Remove from the heat and stir in the milk. Bring to the boil, stirring constantly, then add the nutmeg, and salt and pepper. Pour over the pasta and sprinkle with the cheese.
7. Bake in a 400°F oven for 15–20 minutes, until golden. Garnish with sage or parsley sprigs to serve.

VARIATION
Use ground walnuts or almonds in place of the filberts. Chopped cilantro leaves can be used instead of the parsley.

BEANBURGERS

You can use any beans for this recipe. Serve with Coriander and Yogurt Sauce*, a salad and crusty bread.

*1 1/4 cups black eyed peas,
    cooked
3 tablespoons salad oil
1 onion, chopped
1 celery stick, chopped
2 cloves garlic, crushed
1 teaspoon turmeric*

*2 teaspoons ground
    coriander
2 tablespoons tomato
    paste
1/2 cup whole wheat
    breadcrumbs
salt and pepper to taste*

1. Puree the peas in a food processor.
2. Heat 1 tablespoon of the oil in a pan, add the onion and
celery and fry until softened. Add the garlic and spices and
fry for 1 minute.
3. Mix the peas with the fried vegetables and tomato paste,
then season with salt and pepper.
4. Shape into 8 burgers and coat with the breadcrumbs.
5. Heat the remaining oil in a pan, add the burgers and fry
for 3 minutes on each side, until golden.

Serves 4
Preparation time:
25 minutes, plus
cooking peas
Cooking time:
6 minutes
Freezing:
Recommended

GARBANZO BEAN CASSEROLE

If you sprinkle the diced eggplant with salt and leave for 30 minutes, it removes the bitter juices and reduces the amount of oil needed for frying. Serve with brown rice.

*2 cups garbanzo beans,
 cooked
1 eggplant, diced
1 tablespoon olive oil
2 cloves garlic, crushed
1 teaspoon ground cumin*

*14 oz can tomatoes
2 tablespoons tomato
 paste
2 tablespoons chopped
 cilantro leaves
salt and pepper to taste*

**Serves 4
Preparation time:**
15 minutes, plus
standing time and
cooking beans
Cooking time:
30 minutes
Freezing:
Recommended

1. Drain the garbanzo beans, reserving 1¼ cups of the liquid, and set aside.
2. Place the diced eggplant in a colander, sprinkle with salt and leave for 30 minutes. Rinse well and pat dry with paper towels.
3. Heat the oil in a pan, add the eggplant and fry until golden, turning occasionally. Add the garlic and cumin, fry for 1 minute, then add the tomatoes with their juice, tomato paste, cilantro, beans and reserved liquid.
4. Season with salt and pepper, bring to the boil, cover and simmer for 30 minutes. Serve in a shallow dish.

BLACK BEAN CASSEROLE

This is an adaptable recipe, suitable for all types of beans. I
like it with Endive and Avocado Salad (page 44).

2 cups black beans, cooked　　*14 oz can tomatoes*
2 tablespoons salad oil　　*2 tablespoons soy sauce*
2 onions, sliced　　*1 tablespoon chopped*
2 carrots, sliced　　　*parsley*
2 celery sticks, sliced　　*¾ cup grated sharp*
4 cloves garlic, crushed　　*Cheddar cheese*
1 tablespoon tomato paste

1. Drain the beans, reserving 1¼ cups of the liquid, and
set aside.
2. Heat the oil in a pan, add the onion and fry until
softened. Add the carrot, celery and garlic and fry for 5
minutes, stirring occasionally.
3. Add the reserved bean liquid, beans, tomato paste,
tomatoes with their juice and soy sauce. Cover and simmer
for 45 minutes.
4. Stir in the parsley, then turn into a shallow ovenproof
dish and sprinkle with the cheese.
5. Broil, until golden.

Serves 4
Preparation time:
20 minutes, plus
cooking beans
Cooking time:
50 minutes
Freezing:
Recommended, at
end of stage 4

CURRIED GARBANZO BEAN RISSOLES

These spicy rissoles are delicious served with Bulgur Pilaff
(see page 34) and Coriander and Yogurt Sauce*.

1/4 cup sunflower oil
1 onion, chopped
1 celery stick, chopped
1 clove garlic, crushed
1/2 teaspoon turmeric
1 teaspoon ground cumin
1 teaspoon garam masala
3/4 cup red lentils
2 cups water

1 2/3 cups cooked garbanzo
* beans*
1 cup whole wheat
* breadcrumbs*
1 tablespoon chopped
* cilantro leaves*
1/4 cup whole wheat flour
salt and pepper to taste
celery leaves to garnish

Serves 4
Preparation time:
40 minutes, plus
cooking beans
Cooking time:
6 minutes
Freezing:
Recommended

1. Heat 1 tablespoon of the oil in a pan, add the onion and
celery and cook until softened.
2. Add the garlic and spices and cook for 1 minute, stirring
constantly.
3. Add the lentils and water, bring to the boil, cover and
simmer for 20 minutes, stirring occasionally.
4. Remove from the heat and mix in the garbanzo beans,
breadcrumbs, cilantro, and salt and pepper. Leave to
cool slightly.
5. Using dampened hands, shape the mixture into small
balls, then flatten slightly and roll in the flour.
6. Heat the remaining oil in a large frying pan, add the
rissoles and fry for 3 minutes on each side, until crisp and
golden. Drain on paper towels and serve immediately,
garnished with celery leaves.

CASHEW NUT LOAF

Nut loaves can be dry; this one is full of flavor and moist.

1 tablespoon salad oil
1 onion, chopped
1 celery stick, chopped
1 clove garlic, crushed
1 cup chopped mushrooms
1 tablespoon whole wheat
* flour*
14 oz can chopped
* tomatoes*

1 cup ground cashew nuts
2 cups whole wheat
* breadcrumbs*
1 tablespoon soy sauce
2 tablespoons chopped
* parsley*
1 egg
salt and pepper to taste

1. Grease and line a 7½ × 3½ × 2½ inch loaf pan.

2. Heat the oil in a pan, add the onion and celery and fry until softened.

3. Add the garlic and mushrooms and fry for 3 minutes, stirring occasionally.

4. Mix in the flour, then add the tomatoes and cook until thickened.

5. Add the remaining ingredients and mix together thoroughly.

6. Turn into the prepared pan, cover with foil and cook in a 350°F oven for 1 hour.

7. Turn out onto a warmed serving dish. Serve in slices with Tomato Sauce* handed separately.

Serves 4
Preparation time:
15 minutes
Cooking time:
1 hour
Freezing:
Recommended

VARIATION
Replace the cashews with walnuts or filberts.

SHRIMP PILAFF

This dish is also very good made with monkfish—replace the shrimp with cooked cubed fish. Almonds make a good alternative to cashew nuts.

2 tablespoons salad oil
1 onion, chopped
2 celery sticks, sliced
1 cup brown rice
2 cups water
  (approximately)
1 red pepper, cored, seeded
  and diced

1/3 cup cashew nuts
1 clove garlic, crushed
1/4 lb mushrooms, sliced
3/4 lb medium-size
  shelled shrimp
2 tablespoons chopped dill
salt and pepper to taste

Serves 4
Preparation time:
15 minutes
Cooking time:
40–45 minutes
Freezing:
Not recommended

1. Heat 1 tablespoon of the oil in a pan, add the onion and celery and fry until softened.
2. Add the rice and cook for 2 minutes, stirring to coat it in the oil. Add the water and 1 teaspoon salt and bring to the boil.
3. Cover and simmer for 35–40 minutes, adding more water if necessary.
4. Meanwhile, heat the remaining oil in a pan, add the red pepper and cashew nuts and fry for 3 minutes, stirring occasionally.
5. Add the garlic and mushrooms and fry for 3 minutes, stirring occasionally.
6. Add to the rice with the shrimp, dill, and salt and pepper and heat through. Serve immediately.

BEAN AND MUSHROOM AU GRATIN

You need a soft textured bean for this recipe, to absorb the full flavor of mushrooms and garlic. I like it best with melted Mozzarella cheese on top, but use another cheese suitable for melting if you prefer.

1 1/4 cups lima beans,
  cooked
2 tablespoons skimmed
  milk powder
1 tablespoon salad oil
1 onion, chopped
3/4 lb mushrooms, sliced
2 cloves garlic, crushed

2 tablespoons whole wheat
  flour
2 tablespoons chopped
  parsley
6 oz Mozzarella cheese,
  sliced
salt and pepper to taste
cilantro leaves to garnish

1. Drain the beans, reserving 1¼ cups of the liquid, and set aside.
2. Stir the milk powder into the reserved liquid.
3. Heat the oil in a pan, add the onion and fry until softened.
4. Add the mushrooms and garlic and fry gently for 2 minutes, stirring occasionally.
5. Stir in the flour, then pour in the milky bean liquid and cook, stirring, until thickened. Add the parsley, beans, and salt and pepper.
6. Turn into a shallow ovenproof dish and lay the cheese slices over the top. Broil for 3–4 minutes, until the cheese has melted.
7. Garnish with cilantro to serve.

Serves 4
Preparation time:
15 minutes, plus cooking beans
Cooking time:
10 minutes
Freezing:
Recommended, at end of stage 6

WATERMELON VINAIGRETTE

A colorful and unusual salad that delights everyone who tries it. It also makes a refreshing appetizer.

1 lb watermelon
1/2 cup bean sprouts
2 tablespoons sesame
*   seeds, toasted*

1 bunch watercress
2 teaspoons lemon juice
2 tablespoons olive oil
salt and pepper to taste

Serves 4
Preparation time:
15 minutes
Freezing:
Not recommended

1. Pick out the seeds from the watermelon and discard. Cut the flesh from the skin, then slice it diagonally into wedges.
2. Place in a serving bowl with the bean sprouts, sesame seeds and watercress.
3. Mix the lemon juice, oil, and salt and pepper together and pour over the salad. Toss thoroughly before serving.

ENDIVE AND AVOCADO SALAD

A green salad with a difference. Endive looks really pretty in a salad and has a slightly bitter flavor that combines well with the soft texture of the avocado and the nutty flavor of the sesame seeds.

1 small endive
1 bunch watercress
1 avocado, halved and
*   pitted*

1/3 cup Herb Vinaigrette*
1 tablespoon sesame seeds,
*   toasted*

Serves 6–8
Preparation time:
20 minutes, plus
making dressing
Freezing:
Not recommended

1. Tear the endive into pieces and separate the watercress into sprigs. Place in a salad bowl.
2. Peel the avocado and slice into a bowl. Pour over the dressing and toss until well coated.
3. Add to the endive and watercress with the sesame seeds and toss thoroughly.

PINTO BEAN SALAD

You can use any of the larger beans for this salad, but pinto beans have a particularly nice soft texture and take less time to cook than most.

Serves 4
Preparation time:
10 minutes, plus
cooking beans and
making dressing
Freezing:
Not recommended

1 cup pinto beans, cooked
3 scallions, sliced thinly
⅓ cup bean sprouts
2 tomatoes, chopped
2 celery sticks, chopped

2 tablespoons chopped
* parsley*
3 tablespoons Shoyu
* Dressing**

1. Place all the ingredients in a mixing bowl and toss thoroughly. Turn into a shallow serving dish.

FENNEL AND CRESS SALAD

This fresh and tangy salad goes well with fish dishes.

2 fennel
2 tablespoons lemon juice
2 tablespoons olive oil

2 cups mustard and cress
* sprouts or alfalfa sprouts*
salt and pepper to taste

Serves 4
Preparation time:
15 minutes, plus
marinating
Freezing:
Not recommended

1. Trim the stalks, base and outer leaves from the fennel.
2. Cut each fennel in half and shred finely. Place in a salad bowl with the lemon juice, oil, and salt and pepper. Toss thoroughly and leave to marinate for 2 hours.
3. Add the sprouts and toss again before serving.

SPROUTED MUNG SALAD

If you sprout mung beans at home you can use them at varying stages. If you use them when still quite short, they have a nutty flavor.

¾ cup sprouted mung
* beans*
2 tomatoes, chopped
2 tablespoons chopped
* parsley*

2 celery sticks, chopped
6 scallions, sliced thinly
¼ cup Shoyu Dressing*

Serves 4
Preparation time:
10 minutes, plus
making dressing
Freezing:
Not recommended

1. Place the sprouted beans in a salad bowl with the tomato, parsley, celery and scallions.
2. Pour over the dressing and toss thoroughly.

CAULIFLOWER SALAD

Very lightly blanched cauliflower with celery and a Stilton dressing make a happy combination. If you want a more substantial salad, add some crumbly Wensleydale cheese.

1 small cauliflower,
*   broken into florets*
2 celery sticks, sliced thinly
2 oz Stilton or Danish
*   Blue cheese*

½ cup sour cream
2 tablespoons chopped
*   parsley*
salt and pepper to taste

Serves 6
Preparation time:
15 minutes
Freezing:
Not recommended

1. Blanch the cauliflower in boiling salted water for 2 minutes. Drain and place in a mixing bowl with the celery.
2. Mash the cheese with a fork and gradually add the sour cream to make a smooth paste, seasoning with salt and pepper.
3. Pour over the cauliflower, add the parsley and mix until completely coated. Transfer to a serving bowl.

CURRIED POTATO SALAD

A lovely combination of egg and potato with a lightly curried creamy sauce.

1½ lb thin-skinned
*   potatoes*
2 tablespoons French
*   Dressing**
6 scallions, sliced thinly
⅔ cup sour cream

2 teaspoons tomato paste
1 teaspoon concentrated
*   curry paste*
2 hard-boiled eggs, cut into
*   8 wedges*
salt to taste

Serves 6
Preparation time:
35 minutes, plus
making dressing
Freezing:
Not recommended

1. Cook the potatoes in their skins in boiling salted water for about 20 minutes, until tender. Drain well, cut into chunks and place in a bowl with the French dressing and scallions.
2. Mix together the sour cream, tomato paste and curry paste until smooth.
3. Pour over the potatoes, add the eggs and mix well until coated. Transfer to a serving dish.

RICE AND ALMOND SALAD

A filling salad, particularly useful to serve at buffet parties. The choice of vegetables you can use is endless—vary according to what is in season.

³/₄ cup brown rice, cooked
6 scallions, chopped
1 red pepper, cored, seeded and chopped
¹/₃ cup golden raisins
¹/₂ cup slivered almonds, browned

2 celery sticks, chopped
1 cup cooked whole kernel corn
2 tablespoons chopped parsley
¹/₃ cup French Dressing*

Serves 8
Preparation time:
15 minutes, plus cooking rice and corn and making dressing
Freezing:
Not recommended

1. Place all the ingredients in a bowl and toss thoroughly. Transfer to a serving dish.

RED CABBAGE WITH APPLE

A very colorful winter vegetable accompaniment with a sweet and sour flavor. Ideal to serve with game or any rich meat.

1 lb red cabbage
1 tablespoon salad oil
1 onion, sliced thinly
1 dessert apple, cored and
*   sliced thinly*
1–2 teaspoons honey

2 tablespoons cider
*   vinegar*
2 tablespoons chopped
*   parsley*
salt and pepper to taste

Serves 4
Preparation time:
20 minutes
Cooking time:
20–30 minutes
Freezing:
Recommended

1. Quarter the cabbage and shred finely, discarding the stalk. Place in a large pan of fast boiling water and blanch for 3 minutes. Drain, reserving the liquid.
2. Heat the oil in a flameproof casserole, add the onion and fry until softened. Add the apple, stir, cover and cook for 3 minutes.
3. Add the honey, vinegar, 2 tablespoons of the reserved liquid, cabbage, and salt and pepper. Stir thoroughly to mix.
4. Cover and cook in a 350°F oven for 20–30 minutes, stirring once or twice.
5. Stir in the parsley, transfer to a warmed serving dish and serve immediately.

DAHL

Dahl is a quickly made accompaniment to serve with a curry. You can use green or brown lentils for a change, but the consistency will not be so smooth.

1 tablespoon salad oil
1 onion, chopped
2 cloves garlic, crushed
2 teaspoons ground
*   coriander*
1 teaspoon cumin seeds

1 teaspoon turmeric
3/4 cup red lentils
2 1/2 cups water
1 tablespoon chopped
*   cilantro leaves*
salt and pepper to taste

Serves 4
Preparation time:
10 minutes
Cooking time:
20 minutes
Freezing:
Recommended

1. Heat the oil in a pan, add the onion and cook until softened. Add the garlic and spices and fry for 1 minute.
2. Add the lentils and water and bring to the boil. Cover and simmer for 20 minutes, stirring occasionally.
3. Add the cilantro, salt and pepper, and a little more water if necessary. Transfer to a warmed serving dish.

STIR-FRIED BEAN SPROUTS

This dish makes a lovely accompaniment to barbecued spare ribs. It can be easily varied according to the vegetables you have to hand.

1 tablespoon sesame oil
1 large onion, sliced
2 celery sticks, sliced
2 cloves garlic, crushed
1 red pepper, cored, seeded and sliced
1/3 lb fresh or frozen snow peas
1/3 lb mushrooms, sliced

2 cups bean sprouts
2 tablespoons soy sauce
2 tablespoons dry sherry
1/2 teaspoon 5-spice powder (optional)
1 tablespoon chopped parsley
salt and pepper to taste

Serves 4
Preparation time:
15 minutes
Cooking time:
6 minutes
Freezing:
Not recommended

1. Heat the oil in a wok, add the onion and celery and stir-fry for 2 minutes.
2. Add the garlic, red pepper and snow peas and stir-fry for 2 minutes.
3. Add the remaining ingredients and stir-fry for 2 minutes, until heated through.

JULIENNE OF VEGETABLES

An easy way to make the more mundane root vegetables into a really wonderful dish—ideal to serve at a dinner party in the autumn or winter.

1 onion
1 leek
2 celery sticks
2 carrots
1 tablespoon sunflower oil

¼ cup water
2 tablespoons chopped parsley
salt and pepper to taste

1. Slice the onion thickly and separate into rings, then cut into strips.
2. Cut the remaining vegetables into thin strips, about 2 inches in length.
3. Heat the oil in a large heavy-based pan, add the onion and cook until softened.
4. Add the remaining vegetables and stir-fry for about 5 minutes.
5. Add the water, and salt and pepper, cover and simmer for about 5 minutes.
6. Stir in the parsley and turn into a warmed serving dish.

Serves 4
Preparation time:
30 minutes
Cooking time:
15 minutes
Freezing:
Recommended

POTATOES IN GARLIC SAUCE

Choose small thin-skinned potatoes and don't peel them:
the skin provides extra fiber as well as more flavor.

1 lb thin-skinned potatoes
1/3 lb mushrooms
1 tablespoon olive oil
1 clove garlic, crushed
1 tablespoon whole wheat flour

2/3 cup skimmed milk
pinch of grated nutmeg
2 tablespoons snipped chives
salt and pepper to taste

Serves 4
Preparation time:
10 minutes
Cooking time:
20 minutes
Freezing:
Not recommended

1. Cook the potatoes in boiling salted water for 15 minutes, until just tender. Drain and set aside.
2. Wipe the mushrooms and trim the stalks level with the caps.
3. Heat the oil in a pan, add the mushrooms and garlic and fry for 1 minute.
4. Mix in the flour, then stir in the milk. Season with nutmeg, salt and pepper. Bring to the boil, stirring, and cook for 3 minutes, until thickened.
5. Add the potatoes and chives, cover and heat through for a few minutes.

POMMES SAVOYARDE

A potato dish that's full of flavor—with the addition of a
little smoked ham it makes a good lunch dish.

1 1/2 lb potatoes (not peeled)
1 clove garlic, chopped finely

3/4 cup grated Gruyère cheese
1 1/4 cups milk
salt and pepper to taste

Serves 6
Preparation time:
20 minutes
Cooking time:
1 1/2 hours
Freezing:
Not recommended

1. Slice the potatoes thinly and arrange half in a layer in a greased, large, shallow, ovenproof dish. Sprinkle with the garlic, half the cheese, and salt and pepper. Cover with the remaining potatoes.
2. Pour in enough milk to come almost level with the top of the potatoes, then sprinkle with the remaining cheese.
3. Cook in a 400°F oven for about 1 1/2 hours, until the potatoes are soft and golden.

BRUSSELS SPROUT PUREE

A vegetable accompaniment with an intriguing flavor.
Prepare when you can only get large sprouts.

3/4 lb Brussels sprouts
1/2 cup whole wheat
breadcrumbs
2 teaspoons lemon juice

1/2 cup cream cheese
whipped with 2
tablespoons lemon juice
1/2 teaspoon grated nutmeg
salt and pepper to taste

1. Cook the sprouts in boiling salted water for about 10 minutes; drain, reserving the liquid.
2. Place in a food processor or blender with the remaining ingredients and work until smooth, adding a little of the cooking liquid if necessary. Return to the pan to heat through, check the seasoning and serve.

Serves 4
Preparation time:
10 minutes
Cooking time:
10 minutes
Freezing:
Not recommended

DESSERTS

APRICOT FOOL

It is best to boil dried apricots in water to cover for 1 minute, then drain, to clean the fruit before using.

½ cup dried apricots
1 cup orange juice

⅔ cup plain yogurt
¼ cup sour cream

Serves 6
Preparation time:
15 minutes
Cooking time:
20 minutes
Freezing:
Not recommended

1. Place the apricots and orange juice in a pan, bring to the boil, cover and simmer for 20 minutes. Allow to cool.
2. Puree in a food processor or blender.
3. Mix the yogurt until smooth, then fold in all but 1 tablespoon of the apricot puree.
4. Spoon into individual dishes. Swirl a spoonful of sour cream on top of each one, then swirl in the remaining apricot puree.

SUMMER PEACHES

A delicious combination of peaches, strawberries and raspberries. I often serve this in the strawberry season as it's so quick to prepare. It can be served without the addition of the liqueur, but this does impart a particularly good flavor!

⅓ cup raspberries
2 tablespoons liqueur de Framboise or Cointreau

2 peaches, peeled and pitted
1 cup sliced strawberries

Serves 4
Preparation time:
15 minutes
Freezing:
Not recommended

1. Sieve the raspberries into a bowl, then stir in the liqueur.
2. Slice the peaches into the raspberry puree. Add the strawberries and turn gently to coat the fruit completely.
3. Chill until required. Serve with sour cream or yogurt.

ORANGE CHARTREUSE

A refreshing dessert, easy to prepare and ideal to serve at a
dinner party as it looks so attractive.

4 oranges
1¼ cups apple juice
½ oz gelatin
2 tablespoons Cointreau

1 cup strawberries
1 tablespoon honey
strawberry leaves
(optional)

Serves 6
Preparation time:
30 minutes
Setting time:
2 hours
Freezing:
Not recommended

1. Peel and segment the oranges, discarding all the pith
and pits. Divide the orange segments and any juice
between 6 small ramekins or individual molds.
2. Put half the apple juice in a small pan, sprinkle over the
gelatin and leave to soak for 5 minutes.
3. Heat gently until dissolved, then add the remaining
apple juice and the Cointreau. Pour over the oranges and
leave in the refrigerator until set.
4. Puree the strawberries in a blender or food processor
and mix with the honey. Spoon a little strawberry puree
onto each serving plate.
5. Dip the ramekins or molds quickly in hot water, then
invert each dessert onto the strawberry puree.
6. Decorate with strawberry leaves, if you have any.

APRICOT YOGURT ICE

A very easy ice cream to make, using yogurt instead of cream. It can also be made, very successfully, with other dried fruits; I especially like it with prunes.

*1 cup dried apricots,
  soaked for 2 hours
1½ cups apple juice
2 egg whites*

*2 tablespoons honey
1 cup Greek yogurt
sliced strawberries to
  decorate*

1. Place the apricots and apple juice in a pan, cover and cook gently for 20 minutes.
2. Cool slightly, then puree in a food processor or blender. Leave to cool completely.
3. Beat the egg whites until stiff, then gradually beat in the honey.
4. Beat the yogurt until smooth, then fold into the apricot puree. Fold in the egg white mixture.
5. Turn into a rigid freezerproof container, cover, seal and freeze until solid.
6. Transfer to the refrigerator 40 minutes before serving, to soften. Scoop into individual dishes and decorate with sliced strawberries to serve.

Serves 6
Preparation time:
15 minutes, plus soaking time
Cooking time:
20 minutes
Freezing time:
4 hours

PEAR MOUSSE

A simple mousse with a stronger flavor than you can achieve with fresh pears.

1 cup dried pears, soaked overnight
½ cup curd cheese or farmer's cheese
1 tablespoon lemon juice

1 egg white
1 tablespoon honey
1 dessert pear, sliced thinly, to decorate

Serves 4
Preparation time:
15 minutes, plus soaking time
Cooking time:
30 minutes
Freezing:
Not recommended

1. Cook the pears in 2 cups of the soaking liquid for 30 minutes. Drain, reserving 2 tablespoons liquid.
2. Cool, then place the pears and reserved liquid in a food processor or blender with the cheese and 2 teaspoons of the lemon juice and work until smooth.
3. Whisk the egg white until stiff, then whisk in the honey.
4. Fold the egg white into the pear mixture, then spoon into individual glasses. Decorate with pear slices, brushed with the remaining lemon juice, to serve.

VARIATION
Prune Mousse: Use ½ cup pitted prunes instead of the dried pears and cook for 15 minutes only. Use 1 tablespoon chopped nuts to decorate the mousse.

PARADISE PUDDING

As you'll guess from the name, this is one of my favorites. When strawberries are not in season, use other fresh fruits. The oatmeal gives a lovely chewy texture and added fiber.

⅓ cup finely chopped almonds
⅓ cup fine oatmeal
1 tablespoon honey

1 tablespoon Cointreau
1½ cups sliced strawberries

Serves 4
Preparation time:
15 minutes
Freezing:
Not recommended

1. Broil the almonds and oatmeal, turning frequently, until brown; cool.
2. Mix the honey and Cointreau together, fold into the yogurt, then fold in the almond mixture.
3. Divide the strawberries between 4 glasses, reserving a few slices for decoration.
4. Spoon the oat cream over the strawberries and decorate with the reserved strawberry slices.

APPLE JALOUSIE

Use dessert apples rather than cooking apples, so that extra sugar is unnecessary. The dates and spices also add natural sweetness to the dessert.

*1 lb dessert apples, cored
    and chopped*
⅔ cup chopped dates
*1 teaspoon ground mixed
    spice*

*13 oz package whole
    wheat puff pastry*
beaten egg to glaze
1 tablespoon sesame seeds

Serves 4
Preparation time:
25 minutes
Cooking time:
20–25 minutes
Freezing:
Recommended

1. Place the apples, dates and spice in a mixing bowl and mix thoroughly.
2. Cut the pastry in half and roll out one piece on a lightly floured surface to a rectangle measuring 12 × 9 inches.
3. Place on a baking sheet and spread the apple mixture over the pastry to within 1 inch of the edges. Dampen the edges with water.
4. Roll out the remaining pastry to a rectangle slightly larger than the first. Flour the pastry lightly and fold in half lengthways.
5. Cut through the folded edge of the pastry at ½ inch intervals to within 1 inch of the edges.
6. Unfold and place over the apple. Seal the pastry edges, then trim and neaten with the back of a knife.
7. Brush with beaten egg and sprinkle with the sesame seeds. Bake in a 400°F oven for 20–25 minutes, until golden.
8. Serve warm or cold.

STRAWBERRY NUT SPONGE CAKE

A luscious strawberry cake which is a great favorite with my children and their friends.

2 eggs
3 tablespoons honey
*½ teaspoon ground
    cinnamon, sifted*
½ cup whole wheat flour
¼ cup ground almonds
*1 tablespoon chopped
    almonds*

*1 cup cream cheese
    whipped with 3
    tablespoons lemon
    juice, 2 tablespoons
    sugar and 1 cup sliced
    strawberries*
*1 cup sliced
    strawberries*

1. Grease and line two 8 inch round cake pans.
2. Whisk the eggs and honey together until thick and mousse-like, using an electric beater.
3. Carefully fold in the cinnamon, flour and ground almonds, using a metal spoon. Turn into the prepared pans and sprinkle the top of one with the chopped almonds.
4. Bake in a 375°F oven for 15–20 minutes, until the sponge cake springs back when lightly pressed.
5. Carefully remove from the pans and cool on a rack.
6. Sandwich the halves together with the cream cheese mixture and sliced strawberries.

Serves 6
Preparation time: 15 minutes
Cooking time: 18–20 minutes
Freezing: Recommended, at end of stage 6

LEBANESE FRUIT SALAD

An attractive dessert which is delicious on its own or served with yogurt or sour cream. Any left over is very good served with Granola (page 10) for breakfast.

½ cup dried apricots
½ cup pitted prunes
2 cups apple juice
1 large orange

1 cup fresh dates, halved
and pitted
1 tablespoon pumpkin
seeds
2 tablespoons pine nuts

Serves 4
Preparation time:
15 minutes
Cooking time:
15 minutes
Freezing:
Recommended, at
end of stage 2

1. Place the apricots, prunes and apple juice in a pan and bring to the boil. Cover and simmer for 15 minutes. Leave to cool, with the lid on the pan.
2. Peel the orange and divide into segments, discarding all pith and pits. Add the orange segments and dates to the other fruit and toss gently. Divide between individual serving dishes and chill until required.
3. Put the seeds and nuts in a heavy-based pan and place over a high heat, shaking the pan constantly, until they begin to pop and brown.
4. Sprinkle over the fruit and serve immediately.

PRUNE AND CHEESE CREPES

This dessert is also very good made with dried apricots, or with stewed apples and raisins. They are all sweet enough to make the addition of sugar unnecessary.

1 cup pitted chopped
prunes
1¼ cups apple juice
12 Whole Wheat Crepes*

¾ cup cream cheese
whipped with 3
tablespoons lemon juice
1 tablespoon honey
2 tablespoons slivered
almonds, browned

Serves 4
Preparation time:
5 minutes, plus
making crepes
Cooking time:
25 minutes
Freezing:
Recommended, at
end of stage 2

1. Place the prunes and apple juice in a pan, cover and simmer for 15 minutes, stirring occasionally, until the liquid has been absorbed.
2. Place a little of the prune mixture on each crepe, then top with a spoonful of cream cheese mixture. Roll up and arrange in an ovenproof dish.
3. Warm the honey and brush over the crepes to glaze. Place in a 350°F oven for about 10 minutes, to heat through. Sprinkle with the almonds to serve.

BAKING

DATE AND ORANGE LOAF

¼ lb bran cereal
⅔ cup dried chopped dates
1¼ cups orange juice
1 tablespoon honey

½ cup sunflower seeds
1 cup whole wheat flour
2 teaspoons baking
  powder

Makes one 1 lb loaf
Preparation time: 15 minutes, plus soaking time
Cooking time: 55–60 minutes
Freezing: Recommended

1. Grease and line a 7½ × 3½ × 2½ inch loaf pan.
2. Put the bran cereal, dates, orange juice and honey in a mixing bowl. Stir well and leave for 1 hour.
3. Add the sunflower seeds and flour, then sift in the baking powder and mix together thoroughly.
4. Turn into the prepared pan and bake in a 350°F oven for 55–60 minutes, or until a skewer inserted into the center comes out clean.
5. Turn onto a rack to cool.

SPICED APPLE BISCUITS

Use soft margarine to avoid the rubbing-in process. Don't peel the apples—it adds extra fiber.

2 cups whole wheat flour
1 teaspoon cream of
  tartar, sifted
½ teaspoon baking soda,
  sifted
1 teaspoon ground
  cinnamon, sifted

¼ cup soft margarine
1 dessert apple, cored and
  grated
6 tablespoons milk
1 tablespoon honey
milk and sesame seeds to
  glaze

Makes 12
Preparation time: 15 minutes
Cooking time: 12–15 minutes
Freezing: Recommended

1. Place all the ingredients in a bowl and mix with a fork to form a soft dough.
2. Turn onto a well floured surface, knead lightly and roll out to a ¾ inch thickness.
3. Cut into 2 inch rounds with a fluted cutter.
4. Place on a floured baking sheet, brush with milk and sprinkle with sesame seeds. Bake in a 425°F oven for 12–15 minutes. Transfer to a rack to cool.

DATE AND OAT FINGERS

These fingers are particularly high in fiber as they contain oats, whole wheat flour, dates and nuts. Use dried figs or prunes instead of dates sometimes for a change.

1 1/3 cups dried chopped dates
3 tablespoons apple juice
3/4 cup sunflower oil

1/4 cup honey
1 3/4 cups rolled oats
1 1/2 cups whole wheat flour
1/2 cup chopped walnuts

Makes 14
Preparation time:
15 minutes
Cooking time:
35 minutes
Freezing:
Recommended

1. Grease and line an 8 inch square shallow cake pan.
2. Place the dates and apple juice in a small pan and simmer for about 5 minutes, until soft.
3. Place the oil and honey in a saucepan and stir over a low heat until evenly blended. Add the oats, flour and walnuts and mix together thoroughly.
4. Turn half the mixture into the prepared pan, pressing down firmly.
5. Cover evenly with the date mixture, sprinkle over the remaining oat mixture and press down firmly with a palette knife.
6. Bake in a 375°F oven for 35 minutes, until golden brown.
7. Leave to cool for 5 minutes, then cut into 14 fingers. Allow to cool completely before removing the fingers carefully from the pan.

HONEY APPLE CAKE

Use dessert apples for natural sweetness, and grate the skin for extra fiber and texture.

2 cups whole wheat flour
2 teaspoons baking powder
2 teaspoons ground mixed spice
3 tablespoons honey
1 1/3 cups dried chopped dates

2 eggs
1/2 cup apple juice
1/2 cup sunflower oil
1 1/3 cups grated apple
2 tablespoons chopped filberts

1. Grease and line an 8 inch round deep cake pan.
2. Place the flour in a mixing bowl, then sift in the baking powder and spice. Make a well in the center and add the remaining ingredients, except the filberts. Beat together vigorously until thoroughly mixed.
3. Turn into the prepared pan and sprinkle with the nuts.
4. Bake in a 350°F oven for 1–1¼ hours, until the cake springs back when pressed in the center. Turn onto a rack to cool.

Makes one 8 inch cake
Preparation time: 15 minutes
Cooking time: 1–1¼ hours
Freezing: Recommended

SUNFLOWER CRUNCHIES

1³/₄ cups rolled oats
3 tablespoons sunflower
*   seeds, roasted*
¹/₄ cup honey

¹/₂ cup sunflower oil
1 egg, beaten
1 tablespoon sesame seeds

Makes about 20
Preparation time:
15 minutes
Cooking time:
15 minutes
Freezing:
Recommended

1. Place all the ingredients in a mixing bowl and mix together thoroughly.
2. Place teaspoonfuls of the mixture well apart on a baking sheet and flatten with a dampened palette knife,
3. Bake in a 350°F oven for 15 minutes, until golden brown.
4. Leave to cool for 2 minutes, then transfer to a rack to cool completely.

APRICOT AND ALMOND TARTLETS

Moist and fruity little tartlets, ideal to keep in the freezer as they thaw in about 15 minutes.

FOR THE PASTRY:
¹/₄ cup margarine
2 tablespoons water
1 cup whole wheat flour
FOR THE FILLING:
¹/₄ cup margarine
2 tablespoons honey
1 egg

¹/₄ cup whole wheat flour
¹/₂ cup ground almonds
¹/₄ teaspoon almond extract
¹/₃ cup dried apricots,
*   chopped and soaked for*
*   2 hours*
¹/₄ cup slivered almonds

Makes 14
Preparation time:
30 minutes, plus
soaking and
chilling time
Cooking time:
20 minutes
Freezing:
Recommended

1. Place the margarine, water and 2 tablespoons of the flour in a mixing bowl and blend with a fork. Add the remaining flour and mix together to form a stiff dough.
2. Turn onto a floured surface and knead lightly until smooth. Chill for 20 minutes.
3. To prepare the filling, mix the margarine, honey, egg, flour, ground almonds and extract together until blended. Drain the apricots and dry on paper towels, then mix into the almond mixture.
4. Roll out the pastry very thinly, cut into 3 inch rounds and use to line 14 muffin cups.
5. Spoon the filling into the pastry cases, sprinkle with the slivered almonds and bake in a 375°F oven for 20–25 minutes. Serve warm or cold.

POPPY SEED ROLLS

These are ideal to serve when crusty bread is called for, and they look more attractive than plain whole wheat bread. Sesame seeds can also be used for a change.

4 cups whole wheat flour
1 teaspoon salt
1 teaspoon fresh yeast
1¼ cups warm water

1 tablespoon malt extract
1 tablespoon salad oil
2 tablespoons poppy seeds
beaten egg to glaze

Makes 14
Preparation time:
30 minutes, plus
rising time
Cooking time:
15–20 minutes
Freezing:
Recommended

1. Make the dough as for Whole Wheat Bread*, adding 1 tablespoon of the poppy seeds instead of the sesame seeds. Leave to rise, then turn out onto a floured surface and knead for 3 minutes.
2. Cut into 14 pieces and shape into rolls. Place on a floured baking sheet, cover with a clean cloth and leave in a warm place until almost doubled in size.
3. Brush with beaten egg and sprinkle with the remaining poppy seeds. Bake in a 425°F oven for 15–20 minutes, until golden. Cool on a rack.

CUMIN CRACKERS

Ideal crackers to serve with cheese or, made smaller, to serve with dips or plain with drinks.

2 cups whole wheat flour
1 teaspoon baking powder
1 teaspoon ground cumin
3 tablespoons salad oil

⅓ cup grated Parmesan
*   cheese*
1 tablespoon soy sauce
¼–⅓ cup milk
2 teaspoons poppy seeds

Makes about 30
Preparation time:
15 minutes
Cooking time:
10–15 minutes
Freezing:
Recommended

1. Place the flour in a mixing bowl, then sift in the baking powder and cumin. Add the cheese, oil, soy sauce, and enough milk to mix to a soft dough.
2. Turn out onto a floured surface, knead lightly, then roll out very thinly. Prick all over with a fork and cut into 3 inch rounds with a plain cutter.
3. Place on a baking sheet, brush lightly with water, then sprinkle with the poppy seeds.
4. Bake in a 375°F oven for 10–15 minutes. Transfer to a rack to cool.

BASIC RECIPES

WHOLE WHEAT CREPES

These crepes have far more flavor than those made with white flour. You can also use buckwheat flour, which the French usually use in their crepes.

1 egg
1 1/4 cups milk

1 cup whole wheat flour

Makes 12–14
Preparation time:
10 minutes, plus
standing time
Cooking time:
15 minutes
Freezing:
Recommended

1. Place the egg and milk in a blender or food processor, add the flour and work for 30 seconds until smooth. Leave to stand for 30 minutes, to thicken.
2. Grease a 6 inch omelet pan and place over a moderate heat. Pour in 1 tablespoon of the batter, tilting the pan to coat the bottom evenly.
3. Cook until the underside is brown, then turn over and cook for 10 seconds.
4. Turn onto a plate and repeat with the remaining batter to make about 12 crepes. Stack them interleaved with waxed paper and keep warm.

WHOLE WHEAT PASTRY

A simple pastry to make and far less crumbly than the results achieved with the conventional method; therefore it can be rolled out more thinly.

1/4 cup margarine
1/3 cup shortening

3 tablespoons ice water
2 cups whole wheat flour

Makes an 8 oz
quantity
Preparation time:
8 minutes, plus
chilling
Freezing:
Recommended

1. Place the margarine, shortening, water and 1/2 cup flour in a mixing bowl and mix with a fork until blended.
2. Add the remaining flour and mix to a firm dough.
3. Turn onto a floured surface and knead lightly until smooth, then chill for 20 minutes.
4. Roll the pastry out thinly and use as desired.

VARIATION
Cheese Pastry: Mix in 3/4 cup finely grated sharp Cheddar cheese and 1 teaspoon sifted dry mustard when adding the remaining flour.

WHOLE WHEAT BREAD

A good basic brown bread to start with. Try making different breads by replacing some of the wheat flour with other grain flours. You can also add oatmeal, wheat grains and flaked grains to give different textures, and sesame, poppy, caraway or fennel seeds for different flavors.

12 cups whole wheat flour
1 tablespoon salt
1 oz fresh yeast
4 cups warm water

2 tablespoons malt extract
2 tablespoons salad oil
1 tablespoon sesame seeds

1. Grease four 7½ × 3½ × 2½ inch loaf pans.
2. Mix the flour and salt together in a bowl. Mix the yeast with a little of the water and leave until frothy.
3. Add to the flour with the remaining water, the malt extract and oil and mix to a dough.
4. Turn onto a floured surface and knead for 8 minutes, until smooth and elastic. Return to the bowl, cover with a damp cloth and leave to rise in a warm place for about 2 hours, until doubled in size.
5. Turn out onto a floured surface, knead for a few minutes, then divide into 4 pieces. Shape and place in the prepared pans. Make diagonal cuts across the surface, brush with water and sprinkle with the sesame seeds.
6. Cover and leave in a warm place for about 30 minutes, until the dough just reaches the top of the pans.
7. Bake in a 425°F oven for 10 minutes, then lower the temperature to 375°F and bake for 20–25 minutes, until the bread sounds hollow when tapped. Cool on a rack.

**Makes four
1 lb loaves
Preparation time:**
15 minutes, plus
rising time
Cooking time:
30–35 minutes
Freezing:
Recommended

VARIATIONS

Rye Bread: Replace 4 cups of the whole wheat flour with rye flour; the malt extract with molasses; and the sesame seeds with caraway seeds. Shape the dough into 2 oval loaves and place on floured baking sheets. Stab with a fork in about 8 places.

Buckwheat Bread: Replace 4 cups of the whole wheat flour with buckwheat flour and add ½ cup kasha with the flours. Shape the dough into 2 round loaves and place on floured baking sheets. Sprinkle with kasha instead of sesame seeds.

FRENCH DRESSING

If you cannot obtain concentrated apple juice, substitute 1 teaspoon honey instead. This dressing will keep for several weeks, so it's a good idea to make this quantity.

1¼ cups olive oil
3 tablespoons cider
vinegar
2 tablespoons
concentrated apple juice

1 clove garlic, crushed
1½ teaspoons
coarse-grain mustard
salt and pepper to taste

Makes 2 cups
Preparation time:
5 minutes

1. Put the ingredients in a screw-topped jar; shake well.

VARIATION
Herb Vinaigrette: Add 2 tablespoons chopped mixed herbs—such as mint, parsley, thyme, chives.

SHOYU DRESSING

Shoyu is a sauce obtained by naturally fermenting soy beans with wheat or barley. Unlike soy sauce, it contains no artificial flavorings or sugar.

1 cup safflower oil
3 tablespoons shoyu
2 cloves garlic, crushed

3 tablespoons cider
vinegar
pepper to taste

Makes 1¼ cups
Preparation time:
5 minutes

1. Put all the ingredients in a screw-topped jar and shake well to blend.

CORIANDER AND YOGURT SAUCE

A pungent, spicy creamy sauce, good with pulse dishes.

⅔ cup plain yogurt
1 teaspoon ground
coriander
1 clove garlic, crushed

1 teaspoon tomato paste
1 teaspoon chopped
cilantro leaves
salt and pepper to taste

Makes ⅔ cup
Preparation time:
5 minutes
Freezing:
Not recommended

1. Place all the ingredients in a small bowl and mix together thoroughly.
2. Serve cold, or heat through gently if you prefer.

WATERCRESS SAUCE

A lovely fresh sauce that tastes particularly good with fish dishes.

1 bunch watercress
2 mint sprigs
⅔ cup plain yogurt

1 clove garlic, crushed
1 teaspoon lemon juice
salt and pepper to taste

1. Blanch the watercress and mint in boiling water for 2 minutes; drain well.
2. Chop roughly, then place in a blender or food processor with the yogurt, garlic, lemon juice, and salt and pepper and work until smooth.
3. Serve cold, or heat through gently if you prefer.

Makes 1¼ cups
Preparation time:
10 minutes
Freezing:
Not recommended

TOMATO SAUCE

A versatile sauce which enhances nut loaves, pasta and many other savory dishes. If you cannot obtain fresh basil, use another fresh herb—such as parsley or chervil—instead.

1 tablespoon olive oil
1 onion, chopped
2 cloves garlic, crushed
1 tablespoon whole wheat
    flour
⅔ cup water

14 oz can chopped
    tomatoes
1 tablespoon tomato paste
1 tablespoon chopped basil
salt and pepper to taste

1. Heat the oil in a pan, add the onion and fry until softened.
2. Add the garlic and mix in the flour, then stir in the water, tomatoes, tomato paste, and salt and pepper.
3. Bring to the boil, cover and simmer for 20 minutes, stirring occasionally.
4. Cool slightly, then place in a blender or food processor with the basil and work until smooth. Reheat when required.

Makes 1½ cups
Preparation time:
15 minutes
Cooking time:
20 minutes
Freezing:
Recommended

High Fiber Sources

This table lists the valuable sources of fiber, which you will hopefully find useful when trying to increase the fiber content of your diet.

To give a realistic value, the amount of fiber in each item has been calculated according to how much you might eat in an individual serving. The values are worked out on the presumption that all the edible skins on potatoes, apples, pears, plums, etc, would be eaten, and that any vegetables would be trimmed and prepared in the normal way. All foods are raw unless otherwise stated.

Consequently foods with over 6 grams of fiber per serving are considered excellent sources; those with over 4 grams of fiber are very good sources and useful sources have over 2 grams of fiber per serving.

EXCELLENT SOURCES (more than 6.0 grams fiber per serving)

Item	Weight of serving	Item	Weight of serving
VEGETABLES		**FRUIT**	
Baked beans in tomato sauce	8 oz can	Apricots, dried	2 oz
Beans, dried (including black, black eyed, mung, pinto, red kidney, white kidney)	1½ oz	Blackberries	3½ oz
		Blueberries	3½ oz
		Boysenberries	3½ oz
		Figs, dried	2 oz
		Prunes, dried	2 oz
		Raspberries	3½ oz
Garbanzo beans, dried	2 oz	**GRAINS, NUTS AND SEEDS**	
Peas, dried	2 oz	Bran cereal	2 oz
Peas, frozen	3 oz		
Peas, split and dried	2 oz		

VERY GOOD SOURCES (more than 4.0 grams fiber per serving)

Item	Weight of serving	Item	Weight of serving
VEGETABLES		Figs, fresh	8 oz
Beans, lima	3½ oz	Passion fruit	1 oz
Broccoli	3½ oz	Plums	3½ oz
Corn, whole kernel	3½ oz		
Lentils	2 oz	**GRAINS, NUTS AND SEEDS**	
Peas, fresh	3½ oz	Bread, whole wheat	2½ oz– 2 slices
Potato, baked	7 oz		
Snow peas	3½ oz	Flour, whole wheat	2 oz
		Muesli	2 oz
FRUIT		Pasta, whole wheat (dried)	2 oz
Cranberries	3½ oz		
Dates, dried	2 oz		

USEFUL SOURCES (more than 2.0 grams fiber per serving)

Item	Weight of serving	Item	Weight of serving
VEGETABLES		Pears	1 average-size
Bean sprouts	3½ oz	Pears, dried	1 oz
Beans, green	3½ oz	Plums, Victoria	3½ oz
Brussels sprouts	3½ oz	Rhubarb	3½ oz
Cabbage (red, savoy, white)	3½ oz	Strawberries	3½ oz
Carrots	3½ oz	**GRAINS, NUTS AND SEEDS**	
Cauliflower	3½ oz	Almonds	1 oz
Celery	3½ oz	Barley flakes	1 oz
Eggplant	3½ oz	Buckwheat flakes	1 oz
Leeks	3½ oz	Bulgur wheat	2 oz
Mushrooms	3½ oz	Brazil nuts	1 oz
Parsley	1 oz	Bread, brown	2½ oz– 2 slices
Parsnips	3½ oz		
Zucchini	4 oz	Cashew nuts	1 oz
		Coconut, flaked	1 oz
FRUIT		Coconut, fresh	2 oz
Apple	1 average-size	Filberts	2 oz
Apple, dried	1 oz	Oatmeal	2 oz
Apricots, fresh	3½ oz	Oats, rolled	2 oz
Avocado	½ average-size	Pine nuts	½ oz
Banana	1 average-size	Poppy seeds	½ oz
Gooseberries	3½ oz	Pumpkin seeds	½ oz
Grapes	6 oz	Rice, brown	2 oz
Greengages	3½ oz	Sesame seeds	½ oz
Nectarines	1 average-size	Sunflower seeds	½ oz
Olives	2 oz	Wheat flakes	1 oz
Oranges	1 average-size		

Cooking Time Guide for Pulses

The longer beans have been kept in a dry place the longer they will take to cook. It is not possible to be exact with cooking times therefore, but this approximate guide should be useful.

Aduki beans	40–45 minutes	Mung beans	30–45 minutes
Black beans	1½ hours	Navy beans	1¼–1½ hours
Flageolet beans	40–45 minutes	Pinto beans	1 hour
Garbanzo beans	1 hour	Black eyed peas	30–45 minutes
Kidney beans	1¼–1½ hours	Green lentils	45–50 minutes
Lima beans	45 minutes	Red lentils	20–30 minutes

INDEX

Almond:
  Apricot and almond tartlets 70
Apple:
  Apple jalousie 62
  Honey apple cake 68
  Spiced apple biscuits 66
Apricot and almond tartlets 70
Apricot fool 56
Apricot yogurt ice 59
Avocado and endive salad 44

Bean:
  Bean and bacon frittata 28
  Bean and mushroom au gratin 42
  Bean and tomato soup 16
  Beanburgers 37
  Black bean casserole 39
Bean sprouts, stir-fried 52
Biscuits 12, 66
Brown rice, to cook 6
Brussels sprout puree 55
Buckwheat bread 75
Bulgur pilaff 34

Cashew nut loaf 40
Cashew nut paté 22
Cauliflower salad 48
Cheese and corn tart 24
Cheese pastry 74
Cheese roulade 26
Coriander and yogurt sauce 76
Corn fritters 12
Crepes:
  Prune and cheese 64
  Tomato and eggplant 28
  Whole wheat crepes 74
Cumin crackers 72
Curried garbanzo bean rissoles 40
Curried lentil soup 16
Curried potato salad 48

Dahl 50
Date and oat fingers 68
Date and orange loaf 66

Eggplant and tomato crepes 28
Endive and avocado salad 44

Fennel and cress salad 46
Fish pie, Russian 34
French dressing 76
Fruit. See also Apple etc.
  Fruit with nut sauce 14
  Lebanese fruit salad 64

Garbanzo bean:
  Curried Garbanzo bean rissoles 40
  Garbanzo bean casserole 38
Granola 10

Herb vinaigrette 76
Honey apple cake 68

Kebabs with bulgur pilaff 34
Kedgeree 8

Lamb:
  Kebabs with bulgur pilaff 34
  Mint fricadelles 32
Lebanese fruit salad 64
Lentil:
  Curried lentil soup 16
  Dahl 50
Lettuce soup, iced 19

Melon salad, minted 20
Mint fricadelles 32
Muesli 13
Mushroom paté 22

Nuts 7. See also Almond etc.

Orange chartreuse 58

Paradise pudding 60
Pastry 74
Peaches, summer 56
Pear mousse 60
Pinto bean salad 46
Poppy seed rolls 72
Potato:
  Curried potato salad 48
  Pommes savoyarde 54
  Potatoes in garlic sauce 54

Sunflower-stuffed potatoes 24
Provencale salad 20
Prune and cheese crepes 64
Prune mousse 60
Pulses 6–7. See also Bean etc.

Raspberry yogurt drink 10
Red cabbage with apple 50
Red pepper soup 18
Rice and almond salad 49
Russian fish pie 34
Rye bread 75

Sauces 76–7
Seeds 7
Shoyu dressing 76
Shrimp pilaff 42
Shrimp with almonds 32
Spiced apple biscuits 66
Spinach tarts 31
Sprouted mung salad 46
Strawberry nut sponge cake 62
Summer peaches 56
Sunflower crunchies 70
Sunflower-stuffed potatoes 24
Sunrise sundae 8

Tagliatelle with olive sauce 27
Tomato and eggplant crepes 28
Tomato and nut cannelloni 36
Tomato sauce 77

Vegetables, julienne of 53

Waffles 15
Watercress sauce 77
Watermelon vinaigrette 44
Whole wheat bread 75
Whole wheat crepes 74
Whole wheat Melba toast 22
Whole wheat pastry 74

Yogurt:
  Apricot yogurt ice 59
  Coriander and yogurt sauce 76
  Raspberry yogurt drink 10

Zucchini crumble 30

Photography by: Clive Streeter
Designed by: Sue Storey
Home economist: Carole Handslip
Stylist: Gina Carminati
Jacket photograph by: Paul Williams
Illustration by: Linda Smith
U.S. Consultant Editor: Carla Capalbo